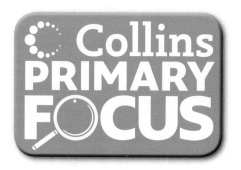

Writing

Pupil Book 4

John Jackman and Wendy Wren

William Collins' dream of knowledge for all began with the publication of his first book in 1819. A self-educated mill worker, he not only enriched millions of lives, but also founded a flourishing publishing house. Today, staying true to this spirit, Collins books are packed with inspiration, innovation and practical expertise. They place you at the centre of a world of possibility and give you exactly what you need to explore it.

Collins. Freedom to teach.

Published by Collins
An imprint of HarperCollins*Publishers* Ltd.
77–85 Fulham Palace Road
Hammersmith
London
W6 8JB

Browse the complete Collins catalogue at www.collinseducation.com

Text © John Jackman and Wendy Wren 2013
Design and illustrations © HarperCollins*Publishers* Limited 2013

Previously published as *Collins Primary Writing*, first published 1998; and *Collins Focus on Writing*, first published 2002.

10 9 8 7 6 5 4 3 2 1

ISBN: 978-0-00-750113-7

John Jackman and Wendy Wren assert their moral right to be identified as the authors of this work.

British Library Cataloguing in Publication Data
A Catalogue record for this publication is available from the British Library.

Cover template: Laing & Carroll
Cover illustration: Zara Slattery Illustration
Series design: Neil Adams
Picture Research: Gill Metcalfe
Illustrations: Stephanie Dix and Emily Skinner.
Some illustrations have been reused from the previous edition (978-0-00-713204-1).

Printed and bound by Printing Express Limited, Hong Kong.

Acknowledgements
The authors and publisher wish to thank the following for permission to use copyright material:

Pan Macmillan for the poem "The Wind and the Sun" by Julia Donaldson, reproduced with permission; Egmont UK Ltd for an extract from *Flat Stanley* by Jeff Brown © 1964 The Trust u/w/o Richard Brown a/k/a Jeff Brown f/b/o Duncan Brown. Published by Egmont UK Ltd London and used with permission; and Penguin Books for the front and back covers from *Goodnight Mister Tom* by Michelle Magorian, Puffin Classics, 2010, copyright © Michelle Magorian, 1981.

Every effort has been made to trace copyright holders and to obtain their permission for the use of copyright material. The author and publishers will gladly receive any information enabling them to rectify any error or omission in subsequent editions.

Photographs
p18: Leemage/Universal Images Group/Getty Images; p19: Veronica Garbutt/Lonely Planet Images/Getty Images; pp24–25: Dennis Lane/Photolibrary/Getty Images; p33: Cotswolds Photo Library/Alamy; p34: Nic Cleave Photography/Alamy; p53: Clive Brunskill/Getty Images; p54: Clive Brunskill/Getty Images; p55, top: Ezra Shaw/ Getty Images; p55, bottom: Mike Hewitt/Getty Images; p56: Mike Hewitt/Getty Images; p57, top: Lee Frost/Robert Harding/Getty Images; p57, bottom: Visions of our Land/ The Image Bank/Getty Images; p58, bottom left: Per-Andre Hoffmann/LOOK/Getty Images; p58, bottom right: Peter Adams/The Image Bank/Getty Images; p60, top: majana/ iStockphoto; p60, bottom: Othmar Meidl/iStockphoto; p61: FLPA/Alamy; p62: Chris Schmidt/iStockphoto; p64, top right: Tom Fullum/iStockphoto; p64, bottom left: Scott Darnsey/Lonely Planet Images; p64, bottom right: Trevor Smith/iStockphoto.

Contents

Story planning

When you're planning a story, you need to make notes on setting, character and plot. Here's a plan Charles Dickens might have made for his story *Oliver Twist*.

Settings

- a workhouse
- an orphanage
- an undertaker's shop
- London – Fagin's house
- London – Mr Brownlow's house

Bullet points mark important items in a list.

Stories can have more than one setting.

Characters

- Oliver Twist: a young orphan who is treated harshly and runs away to London
- Mr Bumble: the parish beadle who treats Oliver harshly and sends him to work in an undertaker's to be rid of him
- Mr Sowerberry: the undertaker – a cruel man
- Jack Dawkins, also known as the Artful Dodger: takes Oliver to Fagin
- Fagin: a criminal who trains orphaned boys to steal for him
- Mr Brownlow: a kindly gentleman who befriends Oliver and turns out to be his grandfather
- Bill Sikes: a criminal associate of Fagin's
- Mrs Mayle: a lady whose house Sikes burgles

give a few character details, not just a list of names

An apostrophe shows who something belongs to.

work out the order of events

Plot
- Oliver is born in a workhouse – mother dies – Oliver brought up in an orphanage
- Sent to work for undertaker – treated harshly – runs away to London
- Meets the Artful Dodger – taken to Fagin's house – sent out to learn how to steal
- Boys seen taking man's handkerchief – Oliver is caught – Mr Brownlow pleads for him and takes him home
- Oliver captured by Bill Sikes – has to help in burglary – shot – rescued by Mrs Mayle – taken to country
- Sikes accidently hangs himself fleeing from a mob
- Fagin is hanged for his crimes
- Oliver reunited with Mr Brownlow – grandfather

Dashes can be used to link ideas in notes.

Think about it

1. Why do you think it is a good idea to make a plan before you start writing?

2. Is this story plan written in complete sentences or in note form? Why?

3. Do you think there will be other characters in the story? Why aren't they in the plan?

4. In the "Plot" section, why aren't we told every detail of how Oliver is reunited with Mr Brownlow?

Now try these

1. Choose a story you've read recently. Imagine you're the author and make a plan for it as he or she may have done. Remember:
   - write it in note form
   - include the main setting or settings
   - give some details of the main characters
   - give the main details of the plot but don't try to tell the whole story.

2. Choose one of the following titles and write a story plan.
   - The Longest Day
   - A Strange Tale
   - At the Water's Edge

   Time how long your planning takes you. Can you do it in ten minutes?

A summary is a shortened version of a piece of writing which includes the most important details.

Here's the opening of *Peter Pan* by JM Barrie.

Note that Nana is a dog employed as the children's nanny.

The children were in bed. It happened to be Nana's evening off, and Mrs Darling had bathed them and sung to them until one by one they had let go her hand and slid away into the land of sleep.

All were looking so safe and cosy that she sat down tranquilly by the fire to sew. The fire was warm, however, and the nursery dimly lit by three night-lights, and presently the sewing lay on Mrs Darling's lap. Then her head nodded. She was asleep.

While she slept she had a dream. She dreamt that the Neverland had come too near, and that a strange boy had broken through from it.

The dream by itself would have been a trifle, but while she was dreaming the window of the nursery blew open, and a boy did drop on the floor. He was accompanied by a strange light, no bigger than your fist, which darted about the room like a living thing; and I think it must have been this light that wakened Mrs Darling.

She started up with a cry, and saw the boy, and somehow she knew at once that he was Peter Pan.

Mrs Darling screamed, and, as if in answer to a bell, the door opened, and Nana entered, returning from her evening out. She growled and sprang at the boy, who leapt lightly through the window. Again, Mrs Darling screamed, this time in distress for him, for she thought he was killed, and she ran down into the street to look for his little body, but it was not there; and she looked up, and in the black night she could see nothing but what she thought was a shooting star.

She returned to the nursery, and found Nana with something in her mouth, which proved to be the boy's shadow. As he leapt at the window Nana had closed it quickly, too late to catch him but his shadow had not had time to get out; slam went the window and snapped it off. She decided to roll it up and put it away carefully in a drawer, until a fitting opportunity came for telling her husband.

(363 words)

This is a summary of the opening of the story.

Briefly set the scene.

If you use words and phrases from the story, put them in quotation marks.

Powerful verbs make writing more interesting.

Include the main events.

The story of "Peter Pan" opens when the children are asleep, Nana is out and Mrs Darling has fallen asleep over her sewing. While she is dreaming about a "strange boy" from "Neverland", he arrives in the nursery accompanied by a bright light. Mrs Darling wakes up and immediately knows it is Peter Pan. She screams just as Nana enters. Nana springs at the boy, who leaps through the window. Mrs Darling goes outside to see if he is hurt but finds nothing. On returning to the nursery, she finds that Nana has trapped Peter's shadow. She rolls up the shadow and puts it in a drawer.

(104 words)

Use your own words as far as possible.

Find a shortened way of saying something.

Summaries can be written in the present tense.

Never copy out whole sentences.

Think about it

1. Look at these details from the story.
   a) "All were looking so safe and cosy that she sat down tranquilly by the fire to sew."
   b) "… and I think it must have been this light that wakened Mrs Darling."
   c) "As he leapt at the window Nana had closed it quickly, too late to catch him, but his shadow had not had time to get out."
   Can you say why these details have been left out of the summary?

2. Summarise these sentences, concentrating on what happened.
   a) Maggie tripped and her shopping basket flew out of her hand, spreading apples, pears, oranges and bananas on the new red carpet.
   b) Sam was very unhappy and when he was very unhappy he sulked. When he sulked he was unpleasant to people and when he was unpleasant to people, they stayed away from him.

Now try these

Here's another extract from *Peter Pan*.
Mr and Mrs Darling have gone out for the evening and the children are asleep.

For a moment after Mr and Mrs Darling left the house the night-lights by the beds of the three children continued to burn clearly … There was another light in the room now, a thousand times brighter than the night-lights, and in the time we have taken to say this, it has been in all the drawers in the nursery, looking for Peter's shadow, rummaged the wardrobe and turned every pocket inside out. It was not really a light; it made this light by flashing about so quickly; but when it came to rest for a second you saw it was a fairy, no longer than your hand, but still growing. It was a girl called Tinker Bell.

A moment after the fairy's entrance the window was blown open by the breathing of the little stars and Peter flew in.

"Tinker Bell," he called softly, after making sure that the children were asleep, "Tink, where are you?" She was in a jug for the moment and liking it extremely; she had never been in a jug before.

"Oh, do come out of that jug, and tell me, do you know where they put my shadow?"

(194 words)

Summarise this extract in not more than 75 words.
The following notes will help you.

1. Read the extract carefully so that you're sure what it's about.

2. Make a list of the things that happen in the extract.

3. Look at the spoken words. If you decide to include some of them in your summary, use reported speech. For example: "Tink, where are you?" as opposed to: Peter called for Tinker Bell.

4. Write out your summary in draft and count the words. If you have too many, check for words and phrases that you can leave out. For example: Tinker Bell was in a jug ~~and she liked it there~~ and Peter wanted her to come out.

5. When you have your summary down to 75 words or fewer, write it out neatly and put the number of words you have used at the bottom.

Stories into playscripts

Well-known stories are often turned into playscripts for the stage or television.

This extract is taken from *Jane Eyre* by Charlotte Brontë, published in 1847. Jane is an orphan. Her Aunt Reed, who has been looking after her, has invited Mr Brocklehurst of Lowood School to interview Jane to see if she is suitable for the school.

Mrs Reed occupied her usual seat by the fireside; she made a signal to me to approach; I did so, and she introduced me to the stony stranger with the words –

"This is the girl respecting whom I applied to you."

He – for it was a man – turned his head slowly towards where I stood, and having examined me with two inquisitive looking grey eyes which twinkled under a pair of bushy eyebrows, said solemnly, and in a bass voice –

"Her size is small; what is her age?"

"Ten years."

"So much?" was the doubtful answer …

"Your name, little girl?"

"Jane Eyre, sir"…

"Well, Jane Eyre, are you a good child?"…

Mrs Reed answered for me by an expressive shake of the head, adding soon,

"Perhaps the less said on that subject the better, Mr Brocklehurst."

"Sorry to hear it! She and I must have some talk … Come here."

I stepped across the rug; he placed me square and straight before him. What a face he had, now that it was almost level with mine! What a great nose! And what a mouth! And what large, prominent teeth!

"No sight so sad as that of a naughty child," he began, "especially a naughty little girl. Do you know where the wicked go after death?"

"They go to hell," was my ready and orthodox answer.

"And what is hell? Can you tell me that?"

"A pit full of fire."

"And should you like to fall into that pit, and be burning there for ever?"

"No, sir."

This is how the extract from the book can be turned into a playscript.

based on page 9 illustration

Scene: In the drawing room of Mrs Reed's house. She is seated by the fireside. Mr Brocklehurst is nearby. Jane has just entered and is by the door.

stage direction taken directly from the story

Mrs Reed: *(gesturing that Jane should approach)* This is the girl respecting whom I applied to you.

Mr Brocklehurst: *(turning his head slowly to examine Jane)* Her size is small; what is her age?

characters in the story

Mrs Reed: Ten years.

Mr Brocklehurst: *(sounding doubtful)* So much? Your name, little girl?

Jane: *(sounding nervous)* Jane Eyre, sir.

Mr Brocklehurst: *(not unkindly)* Well, Jane Eyre, are you a good girl?

Mrs Reed: *(shaking her head)* Perhaps the less said on that subject the better, Mr Brocklehurst.

Stage directions are written in the present tense.

Mr Brocklehurst: *(more stern now)* Sorry to hear it. She and I must have some talk. *(He motions for Jane to come across to him.)* Come here.

Jane steps across the rug and Mr Brocklehurst places her directly in front of him. Jane is looking anxious.

dialogue taken directly from the story

Mr Brocklehurst: No sight so sad as that of a naughty child, especially a naughty little girl. Do you know where the wicked go after death?

Jane: *(nodding yes)* They go to hell.

Mr Brocklehurst: And what is hell? Can you tell me that?

Jane: *(confidently)* A pit full of fire.

stage directions added by the writer of the play

Mr Brocklehurst: *(sounding menacing)* And should you like to fall into that pit, and be burning there for ever?

Jane: *(meekly)* No, sir.

Think about it

1. Where does this part of the story take place?

2. List the characters.

3. How do you think Jane is feeling?

4. What does Mrs Reed think of Jane?

5. What sort of character do you think Mr Brocklehurst is?

Now try these

Jane has arrived at Lowood School and is finding her way around.

I saw a girl sitting on a stone bench near. She was bent over a book ... In turning a leaf she happened to look up, and I said to her directly –

"Is your book interesting?"...

"I like it," she answered, after a pause of a second or two, during which she examined me.

"Can you tell me what the writing on that stone over the door means? What is Lowood Institution?"

"This house where you are come to live."

"Who was Naomi Brocklehurst?"

"The lady who built the new part of this house, as the tablet records, and whose son overlooks and directs everything."

"Why?"

"Because he is treasurer and manager of the establishment."

"Then this house does not belong to that tall lady who wears a watch, and who said we were to have some bread and cheese?"

"To Miss Temple? O, no! I wish it did. She has to answer to Mr Brocklehurst for all she does. Mr Brocklehurst buys all our food and all our clothes."

"Does he live here?"

"No – two miles off, at a large hall."

"Is he a good man?"

"He is a clergyman, and is said to do a great deal of good."

"Did you say that tall lady was called Miss Temple?"

"Yes"...

"Are you happy here?"

"You ask rather too many questions. I have given you answers enough for the present. Now I want to read."

Turn this extract from _Jane Eyre_ into a playscript. The following notes will help you.

1. Look for clues in the extract as to where the scene is set and what the stage will look like at the beginning of the scene.

2. Write stage directions based on information in the extract.

3. If you need to add stage directions, think carefully about:
   a) how the characters speak their lines
   b) what sort of actions and movements the characters will make.

4. Do a first draft of your playscript.

5. Check the draft to see that you've given all the information the actors will need to play their parts.

6. Write a final, neat version of the script.

Themes in stories and plays

When we read a story, we should be aware of the "themes" of that story. Stories can have different settings, characters and plot but have the same theme.

Here's a summary of the plot of the Shakespeare play, *Macbeth*. One of the themes of this play is whether knowing what the future holds is a good or a bad thing.

Macbeth is a Scottish lord who has been very successful in battle. His title is Thane of Glamis which means he is lord of those lands.

On his way back from battle, Macbeth and his friend, Banquo, meet three witches who greet Macbeth as Lord of Glamis *and* Lord of Cawdor *and* as the future king.

King Duncan, the current ruler, is so pleased with Macbeth that he makes him Lord of Cawdor. This sets Macbeth thinking. If the witches were right about him being Lord of Cawdor, could they be right about him being king?

Macbeth writes to his wife about the prophecy of the witches. Immediately, she is determined that her husband will be king and when Macbeth returns home, they plot how they can murder King Duncan.

They invite the King to stay and Lady Macbeth encourages Macbeth to kill him. Macbeth wants to be king but he is not too keen on murder.

The murder of King Duncan is blamed on the guards and Macbeth is crowned king. The witches' prophecy has come true.

> An **s'** shows the owner is plural.

Unfortunately, Macbeth's position as king does not bring him or his wife any happiness. Lady Macbeth goes mad and Macbeth has to murder more and more people as they begin to suspect what he has done.

Finally, Macbeth is killed by Macduff, another Scottish lord. The madness and the murder are over.

Here's a part of the play where Macbeth and Banquo meet the three witches.

Third witch: A drum! a drum!
Macbeth doth come.
All: The Weird Sisters, hand in hand,
Posters of the sea and land,
Thus do go, about, about;
Thrice to thine, and thrice to mine,
And thrice again, to make up nine.
Peace! The charm's wound up.

The witches are casting a spell.

travellers

Enter Macbeth and Banquo

Macbeth: So foul and fair a day I have not seen.
Banquo: How far is't called to Forres. What are these,
So withered and so wild in their attire,
That look not like the inhabitants o' the earth,
And yet are on't. Live you? Or are you aught
That man may question? You seem to understand me
By each at once her choppy finger laying
Upon her skinny lips. You should be women;
And yet your beards forbid me to interpret
That you are so.
Macbeth: Speak if you can! What are you?
First Witch: All hail, Macbeth! Hail to thee, Thane of Glamis!
Second Witch: All hail, Macbeth! Hail to thee, Thane of Cawdor!
Third Witch: All hail, Macbeth, that shalt be king hereafter!

How far is it to Forres?

talk to

chapped

The first witch greets Macbeth with his correct title.

The second and third witches greet Macbeth with titles he doesn't have yet.

Think about it

1. After Macbeth meets the three witches, he writes to Lady Macbeth telling her what has happened. Imagine you're Macbeth and write the letter. Remember to include your thoughts and feelings as well as what happened.

2. Imagine you're Banquo. You see the witches as evil and you're upset that they haven't told your future. Write a letter to a member of your family, explaining what has happened and what you think about it.

Now try these

1. Today, some people want to know what the future holds for them but they don't find out by meeting witches. Make a list of all the ways you can think of to try to find out about the future.

2. Choose one of the following as the basis of a story:

   a) Tom is a keen footballer. There is a very important match coming up but the team will not be announced until just before the kick off. He sets about trying to find out if he'll be in the team and how well he'll do in the match.

   b) Maggie has been offered two Saturday jobs and she doesn't know which one to accept. She wants to find out which job she should take.

   Plan your story.

   Beginning: Set the scene and introduce the main character.

   Middle: Your main character is going to try to find out the future. What method does he or she use? Look at the list you made for Question 1.

   End: How does it turn out? Was the prophecy true? Was it a good or bad thing to find out what was going to happen?

3. What is your opinion of fortune telling? Do you believe in it? Write a paragraph giving your opinion and reasons for that opinion.

Personification

Personification is a kind of metaphor where non-human things are given human characteristics.

Here are some examples of personification.
* the sun smiled
* the trees danced in the wind
* the flames climbed up the house

The Wind and the Sun

Said the wind to the sun, "I can carry off kites
And howl down the chimney on blustery nights.
I can sail boats and set windmills in motion,
Rattle the windows and ruffle the ocean."

> *And the old sun grinned*
> *At the wild winter wind.*

Said the sun to the wind, "I turn night into day,
Ice into water and grass into hay.
I can melt puddles and open up roses.
I can paint rainbows, and freckles on noses."

> *And the old sun grinned*
> *At the wild winter wind.*

Said the wind to the sun, "You'll be sorry you spoke.
Down on the road is a man with a cloak.
If you're so clever then let's see you prove it.
We'll take it in turns to see who can remove it."

> *And the old sun grinned*
> *At the wild winter wind.*

continued on next page

Powerful verbs make poetry more interesting.

The wind blew the trees till the boughs bent and broke.
He bowled the man's hat off and howled round his cloak.
He blew and he blustered, he tossed and he tugged it.
The man wrapped it round him and tightly he hugged it.

And the old sun grinned
At the wild winter wind.

"Take a rest," said the sun. "Let me shine on him now."
He shone till the man started mopping his brow.
The man settled down in the shade of some boulders.
He undid his cloak and it slipped from his shoulders.

And the old sun grinned
At the wild winter wind.

Julia Donaldson

Think about it

1. List the things that:
   a) the wind can do
   b) the sun can do.

2. Read through the poem carefully and write how the wind and the sun act like human beings.

Now try these

1. Copy and complete this chart.

Object	How it can be like a human
rain	
the sea	
the moon	
fire	

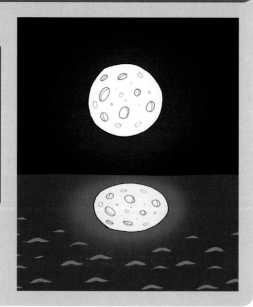

2. Choose one of the objects from the list and write a poem as if the object is human.
   It can have human body parts and perform actions like humans can.

Biography

A biography is an account of someone's life written in the third person. Biographies can be as short as an entry in a biographical dictionary or as long as a book.

Here's a biographical account of the life and work of the famous novelist, Charles Dickens.

date and place of birth

where he spent his childhood

details of his various occupations

details about his parents

details of his education

An adverbial clause shows when something happened.

Charles John Huffam Dickens was born on 17 February 1812 in Portsmouth. His father was John Dickens, a clerk in the Navy Office. His mother was called Elizabeth. During his childhood he moved to London, then to Chatham and back to London again.

Dickens went to Rome Lane School and then Clover Lane School until 1821. At school he was very fond of reading. His education was cut short because his father was imprisoned for debt. Two days after his twelfth birthday, Dickens found himself working at Warren's blacking factory. When his father was released from prison, he sent Charles to Wellington House Academy to finish his education. He remained there until 1827.

Dickens then became a clerk for a firm of solicitors, learned shorthand and was promoted to court reporter. By 1832 he was writing for two journals and in 1833 he became a journalist for the newspaper the *Morning Chronicle*. His job took him all over London and he enjoyed wandering about the city.

continued on next page

examples of his work

In 1836 he married Catherine Hogarth and in the same year he became a well-known author when he wrote *The Pickwick Papers*. From 1837 to 1839 he was busy writing *Oliver Twist* and *Nicholas Nickleby*. From 1840 to 1841 he wrote two more of his famous novels, *The Old Curiosity Shop* and *Barnaby Rudge*.

Proper nouns have capital letters.

In 1842 Dickens went to America. He travelled to New York, Philadelphia, Baltimore and Washington, as well as making a short trip to Canada, where he gave lectures to wide acclaim.

One of his main interests in life was the theatre and he organised productions of plays at Knebworth House and Rockingham Castle.

date of his death and where he is buried

In 1857 he moved to Gad's Hill in Kent and toured Switzerland, Italy and France.

In the 1860s he wrote some of his best work, *Great Expectations*, *Our Mutual Friend* and the unfinished *The Mystery of Edwin Drood*.

He died in June 1870 and was buried in Westminster Abbey.

A curriculum vitae (CV for short) is a form of biographical writing that gives a brief account of a person's life, concentrating on education, qualifications and occupations. A CV is usually prepared for job applications.

Charles Dickens' CV may have looked something like this.

Surname:	Dickens
Forenames:	Charles John Huffam
Date of birth:	17.2.1812
Address:	Gad's Hill, Kent
Education:	1818–1821 Rome Lane School 1821–1824 Clover Lane School 1825–1827 Wellington House Academy
Occupations:	1824 Warren's blacking factory 1827 Clerk to a firm of solicitors Court reporter 1832 Journalist – various journals 1833 Journalist on the *Morning Chronicle* 1837 Novelist
Hobbies:	Walking Reading The theatre Travelling

Think about it

1. Look carefully at the biographical account of Charles Dickens and the CV.

   a) Make brief notes on the kind of information given in the biographical account that doesn't appear in the CV.

   b) If you were thinking of employing Charles Dickens and needed information about him, would the biography or the CV be more useful? Why?

2. A biography is an account of a person's life written by someone else in the third person. An autobiography is an account of a person's life written by himself or herself, written in the first person. Imagine you're Charles Dickens. Rewrite the first two paragraphs of his biographical account as an autobiography. As you're imagining that you are writing about your own life, you can include your thoughts and feelings as well as the facts.

Now try these

Here's a brief biographical account of Charlotte Brontë, the author of _Jane Eyre_.

Charlotte Brontë was born in 1816 in Thornton, near Bradford. Her father was the Reverend Patrick Brontë, a Church of England clergyman. In 1818 Charlotte's sister Emily was born, followed by Anne two years later. All three sisters were to become famous novelists.

In 1820 the family moved to Haworth, situated in bleak moorland countryside. Charlotte began her education at the Clergy Daughters' School near Kirby Lonsdale. From 1831 to 1832 she went to Miss Wooler's school at Roe Head near Dewsbury.

continued on next page

Haworth Parsonage

The sisters' real education, however, was at Haworth Parsonage where their father encouraged them to read widely from novels, plays and poetry and kept them up to date on current affairs.

From 1835 to 1838, Charlotte returned to Miss Wooler's school as a governess. In 1842, she went to Brussels for nine months to study. This was followed by a longer trip in 1843 to improve her French and German.

Her first attempt at writing a novel was in 1846 when she tried to find a publisher for her book *The Professor*. It was rejected but was eventually published in 1857 after her death. In October 1847 Charlotte's novel *Jane Eyre* was published. She then wrote *Shirley*, published in 1849 and *Villette* in 1853.

In 1854 she married her father's curate, Reverend Arthur Bell Nichols but had a brief married life, dying in March 1855.

1. Use the information in the biographical account to write a curriculum vitae for Charlotte Brontë. Begin by making brief notes on the information you will use for the CV.

2. Imagine you're Charlotte Brontë. Rewrite the biographical account as an autobiography. Remember to:

   - write in the first person as this is your account of your life

   - include some of your thoughts and feelings about the various things that happened to you

   - think carefully about the two pieces of information in the biographical account that you couldn't put in your autobiography.

Much of the writing we do is based on facts and there are many different ways of presenting a factual piece of work.

Kate wrote a report on a science experiment and typed it.

why you are doing the experiment

Aim

To find out how much foam is produced by mixing detergent with different types of water

what you need

Bullet points can be used for items in a list.

Equipment
- glass jar containing liquid detergent
- pipette
- test tube
- bung
- 3 glass beakers with
  a) river water
  b) sea water
  c) tap water

what you do

Numbers are used to show the correct order.

Method
1 Half fill the test tube with river water.
2 Add 2 drops of detergent using the pipette.
3 Put the bung in the top of the test tube.
4 Shake for 10 seconds.
5 Leave to settle.
6 Record your results.
7 Repeat the method using sea water.
8 Repeat the method using tap water.

what happened

Sub-headings help to organise information.

Results

Water type	Amount of foam in cm
river water	6.5
sea water	4.5
tap water	10.5

what you have learned

Conclusion

The tap water produced the most foam and the sea water the least foam.

Lynn has written about the same science experiment in a different way.

We had Science today and Mr Simms was not in a good mood. We had to find out how much foam you got when you mixed detergent with different sorts of water. Mr Simms had got some river water, sea water and some tap water. He said he had been to the seaside at the weekend to get the sea water.

We had to get out lots of equipment. We needed test tubes and glass beakers and this thing you use to drop the detergent into water but I can't remember its name. We also had to have a bung to stick in the top of the test tube. I like saying the word "bung". Our bung rolled on the floor and it took us ages to find it. Mr Simms told us to stop messing about and to get on with it.

What we had to do was quite easy. The test tube had to have some water in it and then we put some detergent into the water using that thing. Then we had to shake it up. We forgot to put the bung in the first time so the water went all over and I got wet. Mr Simms wasn't very sympathetic! Anyway, the next time we remembered the bung and we made quite a bit of foam. I think that was when we used the river water but it might have been the tap water. I can't really remember. We had to do this with each type of water and I think the tap water made the most foam.

Think about it

1. Make some brief notes on the differences between the way Kate and Lynn have written about the science experiment. Think about:
   a) the way they've set out the report
   b) the kind of necessary or unnecessary information they've included.

2. Which of the two pieces of writing is more useful for someone wanting to do this experiment themselves? Why? Think about:
   a) which one gives all the necessary information
   b) which one is easier to follow.

Now try these

In the next Science lesson, the class learned about the parts of a flower and why each part was important. This is Lynn's report.

Science again today. We weren't making foam this time. Mr Simms had brought in some flowers from his garden. I think he likes gardening. Anyway, we looked at the flowers and named all the bits of them. I knew the petals and the stem. A flower has got leaves as well. He asked us what the part of the flower under the ground was called. Well everybody knows they're called roots. It was a bit harder after that as we had to learn what the different parts of the flower did. The petals have something to do with reproduction, which Mr Simms said meant making more flowers. I thought they were just there to look pretty. The leaves trap sunlight and something called photosynthesis happens to make food for the flower. Didn't understand that bit! The stem supports the flower and water and food go along it. Mr Simms mentioned something about minerals as well. The roots anchor the flower in the ground and absorb water and minerals from the soil. Can't think of anything else.

1. What unnecessary information does Lynn include?

2. Kate drew and labelled a diagram explaining what she had learned in this Science lesson. Use the facts in Lynn's report to draw and label a flower as you think Kate might have done it.

Journalism is writing and producing newspapers and magazines. People who write for newspapers and magazines are called journalists.

Here is the front page of a newspaper.

THE HERALD

eye-catching headline

ON THE MOON!

sub-heading

And It's "A Giant Leap for Mankind"

by-line

By John Barbour

SPACE CENTRE – Houston – Two Americans landed and walked on the moon on Sunday, the first human beings on its alien soil.

They planted their nation's flag and talked to their President on Earth by radio-telephone.

capitals to show important stages in the story

MILLIONS ON THEIR HOME planet 240,000 miles away watched on television as they saluted the flag and scouted the lunar surface.

The first to step on the moon was Neil Armstrong, 38. He stepped into the dusty surface at 9.56 p.m. His first words were, "That's one small step for man, a giant leap for mankind".

Twenty minutes later, his companion, Edwin E. (Buzz) Aldrin Jr., 39, stepped to

quotes from someone who was actually there

the surface. His words were, "Beautiful, beautiful, beautiful. A magnificent desolation."

They had landed on the moon nearly six hours before, at 3.18 p.m.

ARMSTRONG'S STEPS WERE cautious at first. He almost shuffled.

"The surface is fine and powdered, like powdered charcoal to the soles of the foot," he said. "I can see the footprints of my boots in the fine sandy particles."

Armstrong read from the plaque on the side of the Eagle, the spacecraft that had brought them to the surface. In a steady voice he said, "Here man first set foot on the moon, July 1969. We came in peace for all mankind."

1. Why do newspaper articles have eye-catching headlines?

2. Why do you think the journalist writes "the first human beings on its alien soil" instead of "the first men on the moon"?

3. Why do you think the journalist explains the gravity on the moon and its effects on the astronauts in such detail?

4. Why does the journalist include so many of the astronauts' actual words?

21 July, 1969

Americans first to walk on Dead Lunar Surface

ARMSTRONG APPEARED PHOSPHORESCENT in the blinding sunlight. He walked carefully at first in the gravity of the moon, only one-sixth as strong as on Earth. Then he tried wide gazelle-like leaps. In the lesser gravity of the moon, each of the men, 165 pounders on Earth, weighed something over 25 pounds on the moon.

Armstrong began the rock picking on the lunar surface. Aldrin joined him using a small scoop to put lunar soil in a plastic bag.

Above them, invisible and nearly ignored, was Air Force Lt. Col. Michael Collins, 38, keeping his lonely patrol around the moon till the moment his companions blast-off and return to him for the trip back home.

> information for the reader

> A noun phrase gives more information.

Now try these

1. Make up some eye-catching headlines for these stories:
   a) A lion has escaped from a local zoo.
   b) A local river has flooded.
   c) The football team of your choice has won the Premier League title.

2. Use one of your headlines and write the front page story to go with it. Remember to include:
   a) your by-line
   b) illustration
   c) detailed facts
   d) eye-witness accounts.

   Write a draft copy first, edit it carefully and, if possible, use a computer to make it look like the front page of a newspaper.

How you, as a reader, feel when you finish a story depends on how the story ends. Writers know how they want to make their readers feel and they write the endings to their stories to produce these feelings.

Here is a plan for a story called *The Mountain Climbers*.

Beginning

Three climbers are halfway up a mountain when one falls. He is saved from plummeting to the bottom by a ledge, but his leg is broken.

Middle

The three climbers spend an uncomfortable night on the mountain. The temperature drops and the man with the broken leg becomes very ill. Rescue is a remote possibility because, foolishly, they didn't tell anyone they were going climbing.

Ending

Do you want to leave your reader with a sense of relief?
One climber has a flare so the climbers are rescued.

a happy ending where everything works out

Do you want to leave your reader in suspense?
Two of the climbers go down the mountain to get help, leaving the injured man alone. Will they return?

a cliff hanger ending

Do you want to leave your reader with a sense of "if only"?
A rescue party does arrive but too late to save the injured man.

a sad ending in part but with some happiness

Question sentences end in question marks.

Think about it

1. Write one of the three possible endings for *The Mountain Climbers*. Give the three characters names and help the reader to know how each of them is feeling.

2. Make notes on another possible ending, deciding how you want your reader to feel.

3. Think about some stories you've read lately. Choose two stories, each of which made you feel differently when you had finished them.

   a) Write a summary of each story.

   b) Explain how each ends and how it made you feel.

Now try these

Use one of the following plots and make notes on three possible endings. Think carefully about how you want your reader to feel at the end of the story.

Plot 1

Beginning
The story takes place on a small boat. Two friends are out for a day's fishing.

Middle
Very suddenly a storm blows up and the two friends find themselves in heavy seas, buffeted by strong winds.

Ending

Plot 2

Beginning
The main character of this story can be a boy or girl. The story opens the day before the main character starts a new school.

Middle
Monday morning, the first day at the new school. During the day, another pupil finds that some money has gone missing from a coat pocket.

Ending

Humorous stories are often very enjoyable to read. They're often about things that are impossible but very funny.

This is the beginning of a story called *Flat Stanley*. It couldn't possibly happen – but what fun if it did!

Dialogue is an important part of storytelling.

Breakfast was ready.

"I will go and wake the boys," Mrs Lambchop said to her husband, George Lambchop. Just then their younger son, Arthur, called from the bedroom he shared with his brother Stanley in their New York home.

"Hey! Come and look! Hey!"

Mr and Mrs Lambchop were both very much in favour of politeness and careful speech. "Hay is for horses, Arthur, not people," Mr Lambchop said as they entered the bedroom. "Try to remember that."

"Excuse me," Arthur said. "But look!"

He pointed to Stanley's bed. Across it lay the enormous bulletin board that Mr Lambchop had given the boys a Christmas ago, so that they could pin up pictures and messages and maps. It had fallen during the night, on top of Stanley.

But Stanley was not hurt. In fact he would still have been sleeping if he had not been woken by his brother's shout.

"What's going on here?" he called out cheerfully from beneath the enormous board.

Mr and Mrs Lambchop hurried to lift it from the bed.

"Heavens!" said Mrs Lambchop.

"Gosh!" said Arthur. "Stanley's flat!"

"As a pancake," said Mr Lambchop. "Darndest thing I've ever seen."

"Let's all have breakfast," Mrs Lambchop said. "Then Stanley and I will go to see Doctor Dan and hear what he has to say."

The examination was almost over.

"How do you feel?" Doctor Dan asked. "Does it hurt very much?"

"I felt sort of tickly for a while after I got up," Stanley Lambchop said, "but I feel fine now."

"Well, that's mostly how it is with these cases," said Doctor Dan. "We'll just have to keep an eye on this young fellow," he said when he had finished the examination. "Sometimes we doctors, despite all our years of training and experience, can only marvel at how little we really know."

Mrs Lambchop said she thought that Stanley's clothes would have to be altered by the tailor now, so Doctor Dan told his nurse to take Stanley's measurements. Mrs Lambchop wrote them down.

Stanley was four feet tall, about a foot wide and half an inch thick.

continued on next page

When Stanley got used to being flat, he really enjoyed it.

He could go in and out of a room, even when the door was closed, just by lying down and sliding through the crack at the bottom.

Mr and Mrs Lambchop said it was silly, but they were quite proud of him.

Arthur got jealous and tried to slide under the door but he just banged his head.

Being flat could also be helpful, Stanley found.

He was taking a walk with Mrs Lambchop one afternoon when her favourite ring fell from her finger. The ring rolled across the pavement and down between the bars of a grating that covered a dark, deep shaft. Mrs Lambchop began to cry.

"I have an idea," Stanley said. He took the laces out of his shoes and an extra pair out of his pocket and tied them all together to make one long lace. Then he tied the end of that to [...] his belt and gave the other end to his mother …

Jeff Brown

Think about it

1. What happened to Stanley was really rather horrible. Why is it funny rather than tragic?

2. Why do you think Arthur was "jealous" of his brother?

3. What do you think was Stanley's "idea" for getting his mother's ring?

4. What advantages/disadvantages do you think there are to being "flat"?

Now try these

1. Why does the end of the extract make you want to read on?

2. What other adventures do you think Stanley has where it would be an advantage to be so thin?

3. Because he is so thin, Stanley can do things and get into places other people can't. How might Stanley get into trouble by being so thin?

4. Use the opening of Stanley's story to write a humorous story about something ridiculous happening to you and all the fun you had because of it.

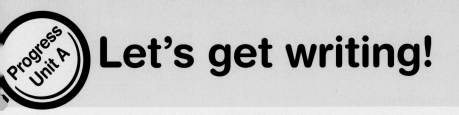

Let's get writing!

Summaries

To do this activity, you need the book you're reading at the moment.

It might be the class reader, your reading scheme book, or one you're reading at home. Photocopy the first chapter.

Read through the first chapter carefully and make notes on the photocopy as you go along.

Use your notes to write a summary of the first chapter.

Stories into play scripts

Choose a story that you know well and have enjoyed.

This may be a complete story – a fairy tale or a fable, or it might be an extract of a longer story.

Write the story or extract as a play script.

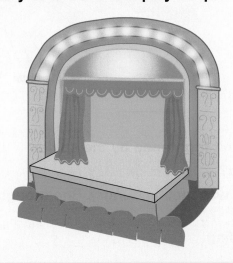

Journalism

Look at this headline in a newspaper:

What could the newspaper story be about?

Write a front page newspaper story to go with this headline.

It could be something very serious or very funny.

Story endings

Read this well-known nursery rhyme.

Little Miss Muffet
Sat on a tuffet
Eating her curds and whey.
There came a big spider
And sat down beside her
And frightened Miss Muffet away.

Now just imagine that Miss Muffet wasn't frightened by the spider.

What happened? How did the story end?

Begin your story: One day, Miss Muffet was feeling hungry. She thought she would have some curds and whey.

Continue the story and write a new ending.

Making an argument

This letter to the editor is one form of non-fiction writing which puts forward arguments for a particular issue.

address of sender

17, The Green
Rainbury
Felsham
FR79 GR9

date

2nd July, 2013

no need for editor's name

Dear Editor,

As the editor of our local newspaper, you should be interested in the council's plans for the village green in Rainbury.

subject of the letter

It has come to my attention that our green is the proposed site for a new development of houses and I am very distressed at the prospect.

objections to the proposal

First, I would like to ask, where are the young children in the village to play? If the green disappears, they will have to play in the street and be in constant danger from the traffic.

Second, the green is the venue for our local cricket matches through the summer months. Without a home ground, the team will have to disband.

My final reason for being appalled at the new development has nothing to do with the practicalities of children playing or cricket. It is just this. The village green is a beautiful spot. It is the heart of our village and gives many people a great deal of pleasure. These days, it appears that we cannot see a piece of open land without immediately wanting to build on it.

correct ending for a letter which opens without a name

Yours faithfully,

Ron Todd

A week later, there was another letter to the newspaper about the new housing development.

From: c.roberts
Subject: **RE: Rainbury Village Green**
Date: 4 July 2012
To: Editor Rainbury News

no need for editor's name

subject of the letter

objections to the proposal

Dear Editor,

I read with interest Mr Todd's letter of the 2nd July regarding the new houses to be built in Rainbury, and I have to say that he has not considered the advantages of building these houses in the village.

My first point is that there is a shortage of new houses in this area. Many people want to come and live here but the older houses in the village rarely come on the market for sale.

He should also consider the types of houses proposed. These are cheap "starter" homes so young people who were born in the village could afford to stay here. There are few houses for rent in the village, which means that many of our young people have to look elsewhere for their first home.

With the building of these houses, there will be more people in the village to support the local businesses. I am thinking of the village shop, the post office and the local pub.

Yours faithfully,

Mr C Roberts

correct ending for a letter that opens without name

Think about it

1. Summarise Mr Todd's objections to the new housing development.

2. Summarise Mr Roberts' reasons for supporting the new housing development.

3. Which point of view do you agree with? Why?

Now try these

Both Mr Todd and Mr Roberts write about one side of the argument.
Choose one of the following proposals:

a) The council plans to put bicycle lanes in the main streets of your town.

b) A road is going to be built which will destroy countryside in your area of "outstanding natural beauty".

c) A Victorian building is going to be pulled down to make way for a car park.

1. Supporting the proposal

   a) Make notes of as many arguments as you can think of for supporting the proposal.

   b) Write a letter to the editor of your local newspaper supporting the proposal.

2. Objecting to the proposal

   a) Make notes of as many arguments as you can think of for objecting to the proposal.

   b) Write a letter to the editor of your local newspaper objecting to the proposal.

Discursive writing

Discursive writing puts forward both sides of an issue, after which the writer reaches a conclusion.

Reporting in newspapers should take this balanced approach.

Television – a Waste of Time or a Valuable Asset?

introduce the topic

The results of a Government survey, investigating what people think about watching television, has been published today.

Six thousand people took part in the survey. They were asked a series of questions including how much television they watched, what sort of programmes they viewed and their opinion as to the quality of those programmes. The final question asked if they thought watching television was a waste of time.

The result was something of a surprise. Sixty-seven per cent of those asked were of the opinion that watching television was a waste of time. The main reasons for this opinion were:

facts and opinions on one side of the argument

- Television has killed conversation.
- Much of what is on television is rubbish.
- Children are generally unfit because they spend too much time in front of the television.
- Violence on television occurs too frequently.
- Television is anti-social and has stopped people from spending their free time together.

facts and opinions on the other side of the argument

Five per cent of those who took part in the survey were undecided about the question but the remaining 28% thought that television was a valuable asset in our modern society, giving the following reasons:

- Life today is very hectic and being able to wind down in front of the television is a good form of relaxation.
- Television provides education as well as entertainment.
- Many leisure activities outside the home are expensive and television is a cheaper alternative.

balanced view of the argument

What can we conclude about the general public's view of television? There is a case for both sides of the argument. While television is a good source of education, it is a worry that children watch so much and the quality of what they watch is sometimes questionable. Leisure activities can be expensive but the somewhat old-fashioned family pursuit of simply spending time together has been killed off, to a great extent, by a reliance on "the box" for all entertainment.

conclusion

As with most things, moderation is the key. There are many excellent programmes on television, in both the fields of education and entertainment, but too often viewers do not exercise the right to simply turn it off. Many people live their lives with the constant background noise of television, no matter what is on.

If television ceased to exist we would be culturally poorer, but let's use it to advantage rather than letting it dominate our lives.

Think about it

1. Which do you think is the best argument supporting the view that watching television is a waste of time? Why?

2. Which do you think is the best argument opposing the view that watching television is a waste of time? Why?

3. Make a list of any other reasons you can think of for watching television and another list of arguments against.

4. Do you agree with the writer's conclusion? Why?

Now try these

Imagine surveys have been conducted to find out people's opinion on the following topics:

- Eating meat is all right.
- The Loch Ness monster is real.
- Sport in school should not be compulsory.

Choose one of the topics and write a newspaper report. You should plan and write your work in the following stages:

a) Make notes on arguments in favour of your topic.

b) Make notes on arguments against your topic.

c) Decide how many people took part in the survey.

d) Decide what the survey showed:
- the percentage for
- the percentage against
- the percentage undecided.

e) Make a draft of your report in this way:
- Think of a suitable headline.
- Introduce what you're writing about.
- Give the arguments for.
- Give the arguments against.
- State what you agree with and what you disagree with and why.
- Come to a conclusion stating that the "for" or "against" has the stronger arguments.

f) Edit your work to ensure you have:
- included all the points
- used paragraphs to show the different sections of your report
- corrected any spelling, grammar or punctuation mistakes.

g) Write or type a final version of your report.

We're asked many times to give information by filling in a form, rather than writing some sort of report. Application forms for membership of an organisation are often required. Here is one for the Tilston Scout Group.

From: c.d.rome
Subject: **RE: Tilston Scout Group**
Date: 12 Sept 2012
To: Harry Jones
Attachment: Membership Form

Dear Harry,

Thank you for your interest in the Tilston Scout Group. I have attached a membership form for you to complete and return to me.

Please note that you must be at least 10 years and 6 months old to join a scout group and you must have the agreement of your parent or guardian.

Looking forward to hearing from you.

C.D. Rome

Scout Leader

Tilston Scout Group

APPLICATION TO BE A MEMBER OF TILSTON SCOUT GROUP

personal details

NAME _____

ADDRESS _____

_____

_____

TELEPHONE _____

AGE _____

DATE OF BIRTH _____

NAME OF PARENT/GUARDIAN _____

(please tick)

previous experience

Have you ever been a member of a beaver pack? ☐

Have you ever been a member of a cub pack? ☐

Are you, at present, a member of another scout group? ☐

information about health

Do you have any medical problems, such as asthma? ☐

If so, please give details. _____

_____

hobbies

Which of the following activities are you most interested in?

camping ☐   reading ☐

cooking ☐   collecting things ☐

hiking ☐   first aid ☐

swimming ☐   music ☐

other _____

agreement of parent or guardian

I _____ (parent/guardian) agree to

my child _____ becoming a member

of the Tilston Scout Group.

I agree to pay an annual subscription of £25.00.

Signed _____

Date _____

Think about it

1. Why does the form ask for this information:
   a) age of applicant?
   b) name of parent or guardian?
2. Why do you think applicants are asked if they have ever been a beaver or cub, or if they are now a member of another scout group?
3. Why is the applicant asked about medical problems?
4. Why is the scout leader interested in the applicant's hobbies?
5. What does the parent/guardian have to agree to?
6. Why is the applicant asked to fill in a form rather than write a letter?

Now try these

Choose one of the following and make up an application form for membership. Think very carefully about the information you, as the person in charge, need to know.

a) a swimming club
b) the local library
c) the local youth club

Poems on similar themes

Choose any subject, such as animals, the weather or families and you will be able to find many poems on that subject. The poets, however, will have written about it in a different way and you, as the reader, will therefore respond differently to the same subject.

Here are two poems about school.

The Loner

third person, observing someone else's experience

> He leans against the playground wall,
> Smacks his hands against the bricks
> And other boredom-beating tricks,
> Traces patterns with his feet,
> Scuffs to make the tarmac squeak,
> Back against the wall he stays –
> And never plays.

the poet thinks the boy doesn't want to join in

form – four verses, rhyming

> The playground's quick with life.
> The beat is strong.
> Though sharp as a knife
> Strife doesn't last long.
> There is shouting, laughter, song,
> And a place at the wall
> For who won't belong.

the rhyme scheme changes from verse to verse

> We pass him running, skipping, walking,
> In slow huddled groups, low-talking.
> Each in our family clique
> We pass him by and never speak,
> His loneliness is his shell and shield
> And neither he or we will yield.

no one tries to be his friend; he doesn't try either

> He wasn't there at the wall today,
> Someone said he'd moved away
> To another school and place
> And on the wall where he used to lean
> Someone had chalked
> 'watch this space'.

Julie Holder

The New Boy

first person, recounting own experience

form – seven verses, rhyming

The door swung inward. I stood and breathed
The new-school atmosphere;
The smell and polish of disinfectant,
And the flavour of my own fear.

The poet is obviously upset.

I followed into the cloakroom; the walls
Rang to the shattering noise
Of boys who barged and boys who banged;
Boys and still more boys!

A boot flew by. Its angry owner
Pursued with force and yell;
Somewhere a man snapped orders; somewhere
There clanged a warning bell.

And there I hung with my new schoolmates;
They pushing and shoving me; I
Unknown, unwanted, pinned to the wall;
On the verge of ready-to-cry.

The poet is obviously upset.

Then from the doorway, a boy called out;
"Hey, You over there! You're new!
Don't just stand there propping the wall up!
I'll look after you!"

The rhyme scheme is regular in each verse.

I turned; I timidly raised my eyes;
He stood and grinned meanwhile;
And my fear dies, and my lips answered
Smile for his smile.

The situation is changed by an act of kindness.

He showed me the basins, the rows of pegs;
He hung my cap at the end;
He led me away to my new classroom …
And now that boy's my friend.

John Walsh

Think about it

1. Make a list of some ways in which the two poems are similar.

2. What do you think is the boy's attitude to the other children in *The Loner*?

3. What do you think is the boy's attitude to the other children in *The New Boy*?

4. How did you feel when you finished reading *The Loner*?

5. How did you feel when you finished reading *The New Boy*?

Now try these

Choose one of the following titles:

- Lost!
- In trouble…
- The last day at school

Write two short poems on the subject you choose. Each poem must try to make the reader feel differently about the subject.

The following notes will help you plan and write your work.

1. Decide if you're going to write about your own experiences (first person) or as an observer of someone else's experience (third person). You may choose to write one poem in the first person and the other in the third person.

2. Decide what feelings you want your reader to have, for example:
   - After reading my first poem I wanted my reader to feel sad.
   - After reading my second poem I want my reader to be amused.

3. Plan what's going to happen in each poem and decide how many verses you need.

4. Decide if both poems will rhyme, **or** both poems won't rhyme, **or** one will rhyme and one won't.

5. Make a draft of each poem. Will the reader feel differently after reading each one?

6. Write your final draft or type it on a computer.

Writing book blurbs

Book blurbs are usually found on the back cover of a book. A book blurb is useful because it helps you to decide if you want to read the book or not.

This is the book blurb for *Goodnight Mr Tom*.

Mum said war was a punishment from God for people's sins, so he'd better watch out. She didn't tell him what to watch out for, though.

> A small extract of actual text gives you a taste of the author's writing style.

*W*hen the *Second World War* breaks out, young Willie Beech is evacuated to the countryside. A sad, deprived child, he slowly begins to flourish under the care of kind old Tom Oakley.

> The blurb introduces the main characters.

But then his cruel mother summons him back to war-torn London . . .

Will he ever see *Mister Tom* again?

> tells you just enough to make you want to read the book

'Everyone's idea of a smash-hit first novel: full-blown characters to love and hate, moments of grief and joy, and a marvellous story that knows just how to grab the emotions'
— *Guardian*

> quote from a book review

MICHELLE MAGORIAN
GOODNIGHT Mister Tom
PUFFIN MODERN CLASSICS
Everyone's favourite stories

Think about it

1. Make a list of the reasons why you think a book blurb is useful.

2. Why doesn't a book blurb give you a summary of the whole plot?

3. Explain in your own words:
   a) "full-blown characters"
   b) "evacuated"
   c) "deprived child".

4. Having read the book blurb, give reasons why you would or wouldn't like to read this book.

5. Discuss any books you have read because of the book blurb. What was it about the book blurb that made you want to read the book?

Now try these

Here's the front cover of a book. Write a blurb to go on the back of this book.
The following notes will help you to plan and write your work.

1. Make brief notes on what the story could be about.

2. Decide on the name(s) of the main character(s).

3. Write a short paragraph about the beginning of the story.

4. Add a quote from a favourable book review.

Desert Adventure

Jack Probert

Extended stories

Many of the books you read have chapters and are lengthy. Writing these longer, or extended, stories needs much careful planning. You have to work out details of the plot, especially the order of events, and how the story is going to end. If you don't, you might find yourself halfway through the book without a clue as to what is going to happen next.

Here's a story plan for the first two chapters of a book called *An Unusual Find*.

Chapter One

Use these headings for planning.

Setting	Characters	Plot
On a farm – kitchen scene where characters are having their breakfast: cheerful/bright/clean, old-fashioned dresser with dinner service, flowers on table, checked tablecloth	3 children: Sam aged 8 – rather timid, scares easily, not sure of himself. Small, red hair, freckles, dressed in shorts and football top Jo aged 10 – Sam's sister, tomboy, very confident, adventurous. Red hair very short, tall for age, dressed in jeans and T-shirt Martin aged 12 – serious-looking boy, elder brother of Jo and Sam. Wears spectacles, dark hair, dressed in jeans and checked shirt	Introduction – describe the scene and the children Conversation over breakfast – what are they going to do today? Reader must learn that they are on holiday at aunty's. Bring out the children's different characters through what they say and how they act – Jo wants to climb trees. Sam and Martin not keen.

Picture the scene in your mind.

detailed notes on characters who come into the story for the first time – physical appearance and personality

make the reader want to read on

Chapter Two

Setting	Characters	Plot
Same setting – kitchen brief mention as detailed notes in Chapter One detailed notes on new characters involve new character	As Chapter One Introduce new character: Aunty Betty – middle-aged, cheerful, hard working, always busy. Wears a dress and an apron. Hair long but tied up in a bun. Anxious for the children to finish breakfast so she can clear away and get on with her work.	Aunty Betty comes into the kitchen as the children are talking about what they're going to do. She suggests exploring and finding their way around the farm. Children agree.
Move to outside, describe farmyard	setting changes – plot moves on	They go outside but can find nothing interesting until Jo spots the barn.
Move to barn – cold and gloomy with rusting machinery, hay, somewhat run down	setting changes again – plot moves on	Jo eager to go in, Sam unwilling. Martin agrees but seems uninterested. Look around inside.
Old cupboard, paint peeling off, looks discarded but is locked		Jo spots an old cupboard in the corner. Finds it locked and decides to break in. Martin warns her not to but she takes no notice. Jo opens cupboard with a piece of metal – strange light and sounds come from opened cupboard. leave the reader wanting to read on

Think about it

1. Using the story plan for Chapter One, write the chapter.

2. Using the story plan for Chapter Two, write the chapter.

Now try these

1. Plan Chapter Three in the same way that the writer has planned Chapters One and Two:

   a) You must introduce a new character but it doesn't have to be human.

   b) You need a new setting – use the clues from the end of Chapter Two to help you.

   c) This chapter can be the final chapter of the story, or you can move the plot on to a place where the reader will want to read on.

2. Write Chapter Three of your story.

3. Choose one of the following storylines:
   - The Visitor
   - The Statue
   - Never Again

   a) Plan the story in at least three chapters.

   b) Write the story using your plan.

Formal and informal explanations

When writing a diary describing your experiences, you can use an informal style and personal pronouns. When writing explanations for others to read and follow, it's better to use more formal language and impersonal pronouns.

Here are two explanations for pitching a tent.

This is a page from a diary written by Tom, a scout at his first camp, describing how he and Sundeep, his friend, pitched their tent.

informal style

informal words and phrases

personal pronouns

uses past tense

When we were given our tent, we emptied everything from the bag on to the ground. There were a lot of different bits, so we sorted everything out into piles. We said to each other that it was a good thing it wasn't raining, or all the equipment would have got wet and muddy.

First we sorted out the sections for the tent poles. There were two poles and each one had three sections. When we had fixed them together, I climbed inside the inner tent and put the pointed end through the hole in the ridge of the tent. By now the wind was beginning to blow and Sundeep was having difficulty hanging on to the guy ropes outside.

Next we fixed the ridge pole between the two upright poles, which was a bit fiddly. We soon realised it was better for one of us to hold the pole while the other banged in the pegs and tied the guy ropes. The last thing we needed to do was put the outer tent over the ridge pole, and before we knew it we could crawl inside and were all warm and snug out of the wind, that is, until we realised we hadn't put in all the pegs along the side. By now it was raining and we got very wet!

This is a page from an information book written for others to read and follow.

formal style

formal language

no personal pronouns

uses present tense

When pitching a tent, all the tent components should be placed on a dry area of ground, or on to a plastic sheet if available. The various items should be sorted so each is easily to hand when required.

The inner tent should be positioned so that a pre-assembled upright tent pole can be threaded into the ridge at the top of the tent. Similarly, position the other pole before a second person outside the tent places the pre-assembled ridge pole between the two uprights and holds the whole structure in position. The first person fixes the guy ropes to pegs positioned either side of both the front and rear of the tent, as indicated in the diagram.

Finally, the rest of the tent is firmly fixed with pegs to secure it against strong winds.

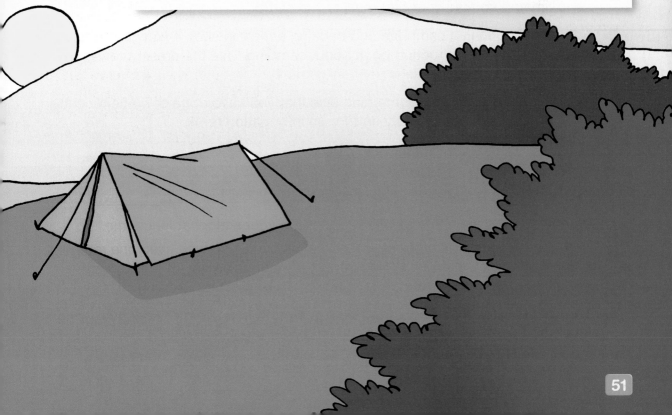

Think about it

You may answer Questions 1 and 2, or you may prefer to go on to Question 3.

1. Write a diary entry, like Tom's, describing the way you and your friend lit a camp fire and cooked your first meal at the camp.

2. Write about lighting a camp fire and cooking a meal in such a way that it can be used as part of an instruction book about camping. Use the present tense and avoid personal language.

3. You may prefer to choose something else that you have done or made recently. Write an account for your diary and for an information book.

Now try these

1. Write a factual description of what happens in your school at lunchtime.

    Start from when the last morning lesson ends and finish with everyone returning to begin afternoon classes. Write a report without using any of these personal pronouns: *I, we, us, me, she, he.*

2. Write an entry for your diary, describing yesterday's lunchtime. Add interesting details and use any personal pronouns that you wish.

Paragraphing

Longer pieces of text should be divided into paragraphs. Each paragraph usually has two or more sentences related to the same idea.

Usain Bolt

Jamaican sprinter Usain Bolt is arguably the fastest man in the world, winning three gold medals at the 2008 Olympic Games in Beijing, China, and becoming the first man in Olympic history to win both the 100 m and 200 m races in record times. Also, by winning the 100 m and 200 m races in the London Olympic Games, he became the first man in history to successfully defend both of the sprint titles.

Usain's early life

He was born in Jamaica on 21 August, 1986. From a young age, he was a very good cricketer as well as remarkable young sprinter. By the age of 14, Bolt won his first school championships medal, taking the silver in the 200 m race.

At the age of 15, Bolt had his first international competition at the 2002 World Junior Championships. He won the 200 m race, making him the youngest world-junior gold medal winner ever! People realised he was a very special athlete and he soon was given the nickname Lightning Bolt!

His running career

Despite being constantly troubled by injury, he was chosen for the Jamaican Olympic squad for the 2004 Olympics but was eliminated in the first round due to that recurring injury.

continued on next page

In 2005, he made the difficult decision to move to a new coach, Glenn Mills. This was a good move but, unfortunately, injuries continued to be a problem.

But by 2007 things were improving. First, he broke the 30-year-old Jamaican 200 m record and then won two silver medals at the World Championships in Japan.

Bolt strikes gold

At the Beijing Olympics in 2008, Usain broke the 100 m world record, winning in 9.69 seconds. Not only did he run a very fast time, but everyone was amazed that he slowed down to celebrate before he finished! He also won gold medals in the 200 m race and in the relay.

At the 2012 Olympic Games in London, he won his fourth Olympic gold medal in the men's 100 m race, beating his friend and rival Yohan Blake. This was not a new world record, but a new Olympic record. The win marked Bolt's second consecutive gold medal in the 100 m.

He went on to compete in the men's 200 m, claiming his second consecutive gold medal in that race, too. He was awarded his third gold medal as part of the Jamaica sprint team.

Bolt expressed his pride about his 2012 performance, saying, "It's what I came here to do. I've got nothing left to prove."

Mohamed Farah

Mo's early life

His ambition grows

British records and European champion

Britain's greatest male distance runner

2012: Double Olympic champion

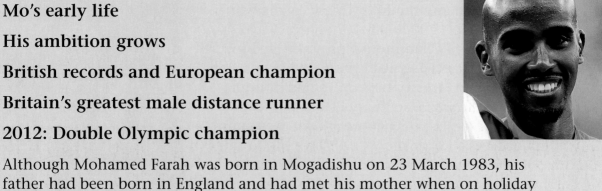

Although Mohamed Farah was born in Mogadishu on 23 March 1983, his father had been born in England and had met his mother when on holiday in Somalia. Mo moved to London when he was eight years old. His first love was football, but it was his speed on the pitch that showed his special talent for running. (More than anything Mo dreamed of playing for Arsenal!) When he was 13, Mo came ninth in the English schools cross country competition, but by the following year he won – and went on to win four more English school titles. In 2005, Mo Farah made the important decision to move in with a group of Kenyan runners that included 10 000 m world number one Micah Kogo. "I don't just want to be British number one, I want to be up there with the best," he said. Soon after he became Britain's second-fastest 5000 m runner and came second in the European Championship before winning the European Cross Country Championship in Italy. The 2008 Olympics weren't good for Mo, but he really started to improve dramatically after going to Ethiopia and Kenya for training. He set a new British indoor record in the 3000 m. Soon after, he broke his own record by more than six seconds, which commentator Steve Cram called "the best performance by a male British distance runner for a generation". However, he became unwell after several races and it was eventually found that he had low levels of important chemicals in his blood.

continued on next page

Once this was sorted out, he started to win more important races. He won the 2010 London 10 000 m in a British record and the following week he won the European Cup 10 000 m and then the 2010 European Athletics Championships where he took the 10 000 m gold medal. 2011 proved to be a highly successful year. In January he won the Edinburgh Cross Country. Then in February 2011, he moved to the USA, to work with his new coach. He went on to win major races all over the world. Dave Moorcroft, former 5000 m world record holder, described Farah as "the greatest male distance runner that Britain has ever seen". On 4 August 2012, he won the 10 000 m gold, Great Britain's first ever Olympic gold medal in the 10 000 m. A week later Farah made it a long-distance double, winning the 5000 m. This was when millions of people all over the world saw Mo's unique victory celebration dance – the Mobot!

Think about it

1. Which of the two passages did you find easier to understand? Give reasons for your answer.

2. The biography about Usain Bolt is set out in paragraphs, with sub-headings, as the writer intended. The information about Mo Farah has been changed. The sub-headings have been taken out and the paragraphs all run together. Read the passage carefully, deciding where the sub-headings should be. Then write out the passage neatly with the sub-headings and paragraphs where you think they should be.

Now try these

1. Write a short biography of a sports person who interests you. You may need to do some research in books or using the internet. Divide your biography using three sections using these sub-headings:
   - Early life
   - Sporting career
   - Greatest achievement

2. Your local newspaper has asked you to attend a sporting event and to write a report. They need about 300 words. Newspapers don't have sub-headings, so breaking the report into paragraphs is very important.

Writing for different purposes

Once you've researched your topic, there are different ways to convey factual information including diaries, letters, reports, newspaper articles, maps and diagrams. The method chosen depends on who will be reading what we write and what they need to know.

Here are three different ways of giving information about Morocco.

The main heading tells us what it is about.

Morocco

Location

The name Morocco comes from the old Arabic phrase *Maghreb al-Aksa*, meaning "The Land of the Furthest West"; Morocco is, in fact, at the extreme western corner of North

Africa. It is the only North African country with a coast facing the Atlantic Ocean, and of all the North African countries, it is the nearest to Europe. The country is bordered inland by Algeria, and for a much shorter distance by Western Sahara.

Sub-headings help to organise information.

Size

The area of Morocco is 440 000 square kilometres (170 000 square miles). This is just a little more than twice as large as the area of the British Isles.

The mountains

Well over one-third of Morocco is mountainous. In the north are the Rif Mountains; further south are the Middle Atlas, the High Atlas and the Anti Atlas. All these ranges, except the Rif, run roughly southwest to northeast across the country. In the east, the Middle Atlas and High Atlas merge to form a barren tableland.

Names of places have capital letters.

(from an information book)

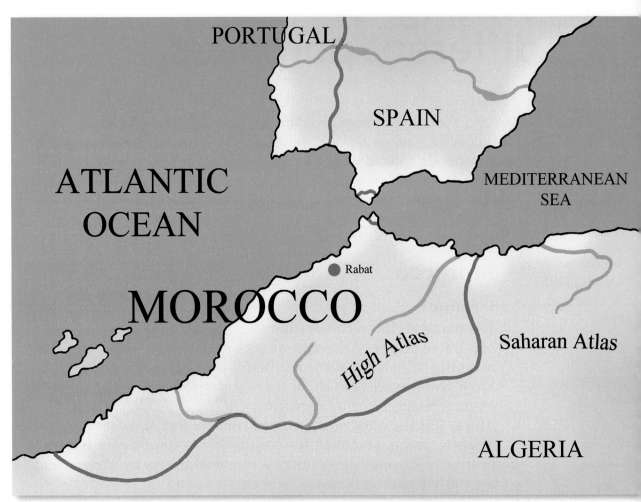

(from an atlas)

Morocco

Population: about 20 million
Main languages: Arabic and French
Main religion: Islam
Capital: Rabat
Area: 440 000 square kilometres
   (170 000 square miles)
Highest mountain: Tidiguin: 2400 metres
Chief produce: fruit (oranges and figs)
   and cereals

(from a reference book)

Think about it

1. Make a list of all the different ways you can think of to give information about Morocco.

2. Morocco is a hot, sunny country close to Europe. Imagine that you've been asked by a holiday tour company to write a travel brochure to persuade people to spend their holidays in Morocco. Think about:
   - the key phrases you need to include
   - the layout of your brochure
   - the most important information visitors might need
   - how you'll illustrate it.

3. Write a postcard home from a holiday in Morocco telling about the best and worst things you've found there.

Now try these

Choose a country other than Morocco and prepare information about it so that you can do three of the following:

- Draw a map showing its main towns, rivers and mountains.
- Write an entry for a reference book, giving as many fascinating facts as possible.
- Write an entry for an information book, using paragraphs and sub-headings.
- Design a brochure to encourage visitors.
- Write a letter home to your class explaining why you're having such a good holiday and telling them about some of the things you've seen and done.
- Plan and prepare an advertisement to encourage people in other countries to buy something that's grown or made in the country of your choice.

Framing your writing

This magazine article has three different types of writing frame. This is because the frame will vary according to the type of information being given. Whether reading or writing, keep in mind the framing that is suitable for the passage.

Animal Rights

a "compare and contrast" frame for the first three paragraphs

In the wide open spaces of Africa, an elephant roams its area, looking for food, bathing at leisure and meeting with other elephants. A dry spell can leave it with little to eat. A pride of lions could attack. But the elephant is free to go wherever it chooses and to be with other elephants.

In a zoo, an elephant paces around its enclosure. It is fed and given water each day. It is well cared for, vets are on call and it has no enemies. But it is not free to roam or to choose its own mate.

Even though the elephant is well cared for in a zoo, many people argue that humans do not have the right to deprive the elephant of its freedom by keeping it in captivity. They believe that keeping an elephant in a zoo deprives it of its basic animal rights.

Respect for animals

The animal-rights movement wants to change the way we all think about and treat animals. They argue that animals have the following basic rights and that humans should respect them.

a "list" frame for this section

1 The right to enjoy life according to their basic natures and instincts. For example, if they normally roam, they should not be kept in a cage.

2 The right to good health. Pets and farm animals should all have decent food and fresh water.

3 The right to be comfortable and avoid pain. Pets and farm animals should not be ill-treated or made too hot or too cold.

4 The right to a painless death. If we must kill an animal for food, we must make that death as painless as possible.

5 The right of their kind to exist. Humans may not destroy all wildlife areas just to make room for themselves.

Different opinions

a "problem and solution" framework for the last three paragraphs

Not all animal-rights activists agree on what animals deserve. Some say that we should not eat meat, while others point out that many animals themselves are meat-eaters. Another argument concerns whether animals should be used to test drugs. Some say that all testing should be totally banned, while others point out how testing drugs on animals has led to cures being developed for many serious diseases. They say that to stop testing could lead to many human deaths in the future.

Neither do all animal-rights activists agree about how animal rights should be fought for. Some believe in direct action, attacking research laboratories, intensive farming units or lorries transporting live animals on long, exhausting road journeys. Others say that this brings the animal-rights movement into disrepute, and that most people will support the case if they lobby parliament, or pursue peaceful means of protest.

What do you think? Do we need more laws to protect animals? Or would more laws interfere too much with the work of farmers and zookeepers and others concerned with animals? These are issues too important to be left to politicians. We, the general public, must decide and we must tell the politicians what we expect them to do on our behalf. Write to us and tell our readers what you think!

Think about it

1. Write a brief summary of what the first three paragraphs of the animal-rights article are saying to the reader.

2. Think of your own pet, or someone else's pet, then say whether you agree with all or any of the five rights of the animals listed in the article. Give your reasons for agreeing or disagreeing with each.

3. The article concludes by asking for the reader's opinion. Write two short letters to this magazine. Write the first as if you were a farmer who breeds animals for a big supermarket chain. Write the other as an animal activist who has been arrested for obstructing the road to prevent lorries taking their loads of live calves to the docks.

Now try these

1. Write an article for a magazine of your choice to discuss one of these issues. Before you start, think of the frames that will best suit what you want to say. Here are some ideas for an article, but you may choose something else if you prefer.
   a) All guns should be made illegal.
   b) Water is too precious to be wasted in watering gardens.
   c) Boxing should be banned before any more boxers become brain-damaged.

2. Find out the name of your MP and write and send a letter saying how you feel about the issue you chose in Question 1. Address it to the House of Commons, London, SW1A 0AA.

3. Make either a poster **or** a leaflet in support of your cause. Think about the main points you want to make and write some strong, catchy phrases that will stick in people's minds. Design the poster or leaflet so that it is attractive and clear.

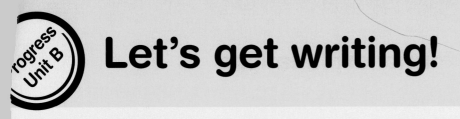
Let's get writing!

Book blurbs

Look back at the story you wrote for Little Miss Muffet when you changed the ending.

Imagine this story was published for younger children.

Write a book blurb aimed at parents who might buy the book for their children.

Extended stories

Turn to page 43 and read the poem *The New Boy* again.

Imagine that this was written in prose.

What happens in the poem is Chapter 1, which is called "Arriving At School".

Make a plan of the next two chapters.

- Chapter 2: The First Day
- Chapter 3: Back At Home

Formal and informal explanations

Choose one of the following:

1. mending a puncture in your bicycle tyre

2. helping to prepare and pack a picnic

Write:

- a formal explanation of how you would go about doing it
- a letter to a friend about it.

Paragraphing

Research one of the following:

1. three different types of cloud
2. three famous explorers
3. three types of cars

Present your information in three paragraphs.